TOUCHSTONES
VOLUME C
Texts for Discussion

Selected, translated, and edited
by
Geoffrey Comber
Howard Zeiderman
Nicholas Maistrellis

Published by
TOUCHSTONES
DISCUSSION PROJECT

About the Touchstones Discussion Project

The Touchstones Discussion Project is a nonprofit organization founded on the belief that all people can benefit from the listening, speaking, thinking, and interpersonal skills gained by engaging in active, focused discussions. Since 1984, Touchstones has helped millions of students and others develop and improve these skills in school, work, and life. For more information about the Touchstones Discussion Project, visit www.touchstones.org.

Touchstones Discussion Project
PO Box 2329
Annapolis, Maryland 21404
800-456-6542
www.touchstones.org

©1996, 2002 by Touchstones Discussion Project.
All rights reserved. No part of this book may be reproduced in any form without prior consent of the publisher.

ISBN: 1-878461-61-3

ACKNOWLEDGEMENTS

We would like to thank the National Gallery of Art, Washington D.C., for permission to reproduce the following:

Woman Holding a Balance, by Jan Vermeer, Widener Collection

Prisoners Listening to Music, by Käthe Kollwitz, Rosenwald Collection.

CONTENTS

INTRODUCTION ix

1. The Orientation Class 1

2. The Republic
    by Plato 5

3. Of Anger
    by Francis Bacon 9

4. On Human Cures for Sadness
    by St. Thomas Aquinas 11

5. God, Death and the Hungry Peasant
    A Mexican Folktale 13

6. Two Different Kinds of Minds
    by Pascal 17

7. The Histories
    by Herodotus 19

8. A Mathematician's Defense
    by G. H. Hardy 21

9. Democracy in America "Equality and Liberty"
   by A. de Tocqueville 23

10. The Consolation of Philosophy
    by Boethius 25

11. Declaration of Independence
    (Opening Paragraphs) 27

12. On Public Education
    by Thomas Jefferson 29

13. Continuity and Irrational Numbers
    by Richard Dedekind 31

14. Character
    by Voltaire 33

15. On Moral Education
    by Horace Mann 35

16. The Notebooks
    by Leonardo da Vinci 37

17. Article One of the Amendments to
    the Constitution of the United States. 39

18. On Religion and the State
    by Thomas Jefferson 41

19. Federalist Paper No. 10
    by James Madison 43

20. Federalist Paper No. 2
    by John Jay 47

21. Democracy in America "Why Americans are so Restless"
    by Alexis de Tocqueville 49

22. The Meno
    by Plato 51

23. Prisoners Listening to Music
     Kathe Kollwitz 53

24. To Emancipate the Mind
     by Abraham Lincoln, 1859 55

25. Bonifacius—Essays to Do Good
     by Cotton Mather 59

26. Emile or On Education
     by Jean-Jacques Rousseau 61

27. Open Letter to his Former Master
     by Frederick Douglass 63

28. The Life of Alcibiades
     by Plutarch 65

29. Woman Holding a Balance
     by Jan Vermeer 67

30. We Cannot Live for Ourselves Alone
     by Vernon E. Jordan Jr. 69

INTRODUCTION

As the world changes, so must change the ways we teach and learn. Our world is becoming more interconnected, bringing together people with diverse backgrounds and differing perspectives. Technology places volumes of information at our fingertips. Such skills as problem-solving in groups, processing and evaluating new information, and working with diverse groups of people are more critical than ever to students' success. Students must now also learn how to teach themselves.

The Touchstones Discussion Project offers students and teachers the tools to meet the demands of this emerging environment. Students of all backgrounds and skill levels, across the United States and around the world, currently participate in Touchstones. In their weekly Touchstones Discussion classes, students learn strategies to help them navigate their way through school and through life. Touchstones helps students learn to process information, ask the right questions, and enlist the help of others in making decisions. As they listen, explore, cooperate, and solve problems, they become true collaborators in their own learning. They learn that life is not always about answers being right or wrong but rather about decisions being better or worse.

Not only do students learn how to learn, teachers learn a new way to teach. The Touchstones Method offers teachers a powerful, new approach to group discussion that results in fully active and eager participation by the students. Eventually, the students themselves take the lead in the process. By bridging the gap between students' schoolwork and their experiences outside of school, Touchstones Discussions bring the classroom to life.

Skills

Touchstones Discussions develop skills that students will use in all their classes, and they help students create a more responsible attitude toward their entire education. Examples of these skills and attitudes include the following:

- Cooperating with their classmates, regardless of background
- Stating ideas clearly
- Respecting others' opinions
- Identifying key issues of topics and texts
- Asking questions to clarify discussion and improve understanding
- Integrating text with experience and prior knowledge
- Formulating complex ideas
- Supporting opinions with evidence
- Using questioning strategies
- Exploring various interpretations of a text
- Confronting difficult problems that do not have clear right and wrong answers

Touchstones Classes and the Texts

Typically, a class in the Touchstones Discussion Project has the following parts and shape:

- Students do not prepare before class.
- The whole class, including the teacher, sits in a circle.
- The teacher reads the text aloud as students follow along silently.
- Students do individual work.
- Students do small group work.
- The teacher asks an open-ended question to start discussion.
- Students do not raise their hands.
- Ground rules are followed.

The thirty texts in this volume are drawn from a wide variety of authors—male, female, minorities—from a wide variety of cultures. This variety allows and encourages students to experiment with different perspectives and alternative points of view, and allows them to apply the textual material to their own lives.

Students begin to ask not only "What does the author really mean by this passage?" but also "How does this text apply to my life?"

The Role of the Teacher

The teacher's role in working with the Touchstones Discussion Project is noticeably different from the teacher's role in other classes, especially in relation to the whole class discussions. The main point for teachers to keep in mind is that, in these Touchstones classes, teachers are not imparting information or knowledge but instead are cultivating skills and promoting attitudinal changes in the students. This means that teachers should resist the temptation to give background information about authors or cultures and should not praise or correct students with regarding their opinions about the texts. Rather, the proper role is to try to generate those conditions, suggested by the exercises for each of the classes outlined in the Teacher's Guide, that help students cooperate, produce fertile uses for the texts, and view serious texts as "friendly." Nevertheless, teachers are still teachers with responsibilities, and discipline problems should be dealt with in whatever manner is usual and effective.

Organization of the Room

Touchstones classes never take place in a room with chairs or desks arranged in the familiar rows, where most students only see the back of the head of the student in front of them. Instead, chairs usually need to be moved at least three times in the course of the period: first, to form a single circle; second, to form groups of three to five; and third, to reform a large circle. Cooperation can occur only when facing the people one is trying to cooperate with, whether that is three, four, or twenty-nine other students. Reasonably accurate circles also make it harder for pairs of students to have side conversations while another student is explaining what he or she believes. Side conversations are an act of disrespect, and they inhibit the mutual respect Touchstones Discussions try to foster. Touchstones classes use many such devices to instill the mutual and self-respect that lead to cooperation.

And respect and cooperation are major steps toward taking responsibility for teaching others and oneself.

Teacher's Guides

The Teacher's Guide for this volume contains information to help teachers make the most of Touchstones Discussions. Each lesson includes the following:
- Purpose statement for the lesson
- Introduction to the lesson
- Summary of the text
- Possible question for discussion
- Detailed lesson plan
- Student worksheets for individual and small group work

The Teacher's Guides also includes a variety of tools to help teachers throughout the year, including benchmarks and evaluation sheets that help teachers plan for each lesson and evaluate the group's strengths and weaknesses.

Additional support is available through Touchstones teacher workshops, the Touchstones Web site at www.touchstones.org, or by calling our office at 800-456-6542.

The Orientation Class

You, your classmates, and your teacher are about to begin a class which differs in some ways from your regular classes. The purpose of this class is to enable you to gain certain skills that will help you profit more from your regular classes. The new class is a discussion class. You will be talking to one another as well as to your teacher. We are all familiar with discussions because we have all discussed problems, feelings, opinions, and experiences with friends and relatives all of our lives. However, the discussions you will have in this class differ in some ways from your previous experiences.

Unlike your regular classes, in Touchstones discussion classes,

a. everyone sits in a circle,

b. the teacher is a member of the group and will help, but isn't an authority with the correct answers,

c. there is no hand raising, instead everyone will learn how to run the discussion, and

d. there is no preparation.

Unlike discussions which happen outside of class with friends and relatives, in Touchstones classes,

a. discussions involve everyone in the class, your friends as well as students you don't know very well,

b. discussions are about readings from the Touchstones book and not just our own concerns and experiences, and

c. discussions occur once a week at a scheduled time, begin with a question asked by the teacher, and end when the teacher decides or when the bell rings.

Because of these differences, everyone must follow certain ground rules.

GROUND RULES

1. **Read the Text Carefully.** In Touchstones discussions your opinions are important, but these opinions are your thoughts about the text.
2. **Listen to What Others Say and Don't Interrupt.** A discussion cannot occur if you don't listen carefully to what people say.
3. **Speak Clearly.** For others to respond to your opinions, everyone must be able to hear and understand you.
4. **Give Others Your Respect.** A discussion is a cooperative exchange of ideas and not an argument or a debate. You may become excited and wish to share your ideas, but don't talk privately to your neighbor. In a Touchstones class, you will talk publicly for the whole class.

GOALS: WHAT YOU CAN GAIN FROM TOUCHSTONES DISCUSSION CLASSES

You will learn to:

a. listen better to what others say,

b. explain you own ideas,

c. speak and work with others whether you know them or not,

d. receive correction and criticism from others,

e. ask about what you don't understand,

f. admit when you're wrong,

g. think about questions for which the answers are uncertain,

h. learn from others,

i. teach others,

j. teach yourself, and

k. become more aware of how others see you.

The Republic
by Plato

"Is there any way for us to understand a little better how we come to learn what things are true?" asked Glaucon.

"Yes," replied Socrates. "I will tell you a story that will show how we move from a state of ignorance to knowledge.

"Imagine a large cave deep underground with only one exit to the light. Next imagine at the deepest part of the cave there are men who have been living there since early childhood. They are chained so that they can only look at one wall of the cave, and they cannot turn their heads round to see what is behind them. But in fact there is a fire burning behind and above them, and it casts shadows of objects on the wall of the cave. However, the prisoners can only see the shadows moving in front of them. They don't know about the fire and therefore think these shadows are the real things.

"This is a strange story and they are strange prisoners," said Glaucon.

"They are actually not all that different from us," said Socrates. "At first they, like us, see shapes moving, and hear sounds that seem to be coming from them. And if the prisoners talked to each other about what they saw and heard, they would think they were talking about real things. But in fact their words would be about shadows."

"That's right," agreed Glaucon. "What else could they think?"

"Now imagine that somehow, we don't know how, one of the prisoners was released from his chains. Imagine he was forced to stand up and turn round to face the fire. This would be very painful at first. And he would be very confused when, all at once, he saw the shadows, the fire, and some objects that were similar to the shadows. He would not know which was more real. He would be so uncomfortable that he would probably try to go back to his original place where he was chained because at least that was familiar to him.

"But suppose he was not allowed to return to where he had been and instead was forced to climb up the slope of the cave until he was out in the sunlight. Would he not be angry and suffer a great deal of pain as his eyes were hurt by the bright light?"

"Of course. It would be painful and he wouldn't know what to make of it," said Glaucon.

"Gradually, if he worked at it, his eyes would see the shadows of trees and other objects. Then he would be able to look at the trees and the animals themselves. Finally he would be able to look at the sky and the sun. He would now be able to understand the relations among the shadows on the cave wall, the fire and the objects casting the shadows, and the sun which is the cause of everything. I say that this man's adventures are just like ours as we gain a greater understanding about reality. It is painful and it is hard work.

"But now that he saw how things really are, he would be happy and feel sorry for the prisoners who were still chained in the cave below. He would go back into the cave to tell them how the world really is–so much greater than the little world of the cave wall that they knew. How do you think they would treat him?"

 Of Anger
by Francis Bacon

Anger cannot be completely stamped out, but it can be controlled and calmed. We will speak first about how the tendency or habit to be angry can be changed or softened; secondly, about how to prevent anger from causing further harm.

For the first, there is no other way but to think deeply about how much being angry disturbs, troubles, and throws your life into turmoil. The best time to do this is when the fit of anger is thoroughly over. The Bible urges us to try and be more patient. When people lose their patience, they lose possession of their souls.

For the second point, there are three main causes and motives of anger. The first is being hurt too easily—for no one is angry unless he or she feels hurt. Therefore, weak, soft, and delicate persons often become angry. They have so many things to trouble them of which stronger people are not even aware. The second main cause is if, in addition to feeling a hurt, the hurt is combined with hatred. For hatred can cause anger as much or more than the hurt itself. Lastly, anger becomes much sharper if a person's reputation is touched or even spoken about. The best cure for this is to have a tougher hide. But the best way to prevent getting angry is to gain time. Make yourself believe that now is not the best time to get even, but later will be better. In the meantime, you can calm down.

There are two things you should be very careful about if you lose your temper. The first is not to say anything you will regret, such as bitter and spiteful words, especially if they are true. Also never reveal a secret. The other is that you should not end any matter in anger. Never take any action which cannot ever be changed back again into how it was before.

On Human Cures for Sadness
by St. Thomas Aquinas

Question: Are there any human cures for sadness?

Answer: There are some sorrows that only God can take away. Still, human beings were made to be happy. They were not made to be sad. So there are things human beings can do to cure sadness. Here are five cures for sadness:

1. Any delightful activity—for sadness is to the soul as weariness is to the body. Delightful activity is like rest for the soul.

2. Tears.

3. The compassion of friends.

4. Learning what is true about the world—this seems to help some people more than it helps others.

5. Bathing and sleeping—for when your body feels better, your soul will feel better too.

To say more about the third point, let me ask whether the compassion of friends is a cure for sadness. Some people don't think so. Here are some arguments.

1. It would seem that sadness isn't cured by the compassion of friends. As Saint Augustine says, "When many people are celebrating together, the pleasure of each one is greater than it would be if each were alone." In the same way, when many people are

sad together, the sadness of each is greater than it would be if each were alone.

2. Friends, as Saint Augustine says, repay love with love. But a friend who is being compassionate because of his friend's sadness also himself becomes sad. His sadness makes the friend he was trying to cure even sadder. Therefore, the compassion of friends is not a cure for sadness.

On the other hand, I say that everyone knows from experience that when we are sad, the compassion of friends helps. Aristotle says that there are two reasons for this. First, sadness is like a weight which we are carrying. When friends are being compassionate, they are helping us to carry this weight. They are making it lighter for us.

Aristotle's second reason is even better. When a person's friends share his sadness, that person sees that his friends love him. This fact is a source of pleasure. But pleasure, as we have already said, eases pain. It follows, therefore, that sadness is eased when friends share it.

My answers to the two arguments above are the following:

3. When a person shares in our joy or in our sadness, he is showing friendship. In both cases, friendship gives us pleasure. It is this pleasure which helps to take away sadness.

4. It is true that a friend's sadness, because of our sadness, adds to our sadness. However, there is also pleasure because we realize that the friend loves us.

God, Death and the Hungry Peasant
A Mexican Folktale

Near Xoaxaca there lived a poor peasant. His farm was so small, and the soil so bad, that it never produced enough to feed his family. He, his wife, and his children were always very hungry, even though he worked hard. For the last few weeks, he had to give up more and more of his own food to keep his family from starving.

One day, he stole a chicken. He thought he would go way up into the hills where he could cook it and eat it all by himself. He found a quiet spot in the hills where no one could see him, made a fire, put the chicken in a pot with some water from a stream, and cooked it. Just when the chicken was ready and he was about to eat, he saw someone coming along a footpath toward him. The peasant quickly hid the pot in some bushes.

The stranger greeted him.

"Hello, my friend. What are you doing here?"

"Nothing, señor. Just taking a rest. Where are you going?"

"I saw some smoke and came to ask you for something to eat," said the stranger.

"I haven't got anything, señor," replied the peasant.

"But you have a fire burning."

"Oh, this is just to keep myself warm," the peasant answered.

"I can smell chicken cooking," the stranger said. "You must have a pot hidden in those bushes."

"Well, yes, I have. But I'm not giving you any," the peasant complained. "I'm not even giving my wife and children any. I haven't eaten for many days, and this is all for me."

"Come, my friend," said the stranger. "Give me just a little piece. You don't know who I am."

The peasant answered, "I don't care who you are. I am not giving you any."

The stranger drew himself up and said, "You will when I tell you who I am."

"Well then, who are you?"

"I am the Lord, your God."

But the peasant cried out, "Now I'm certain I will never share my food with you. You're always bad to the poor people. You give palaces and horses and cattle and coaches and lots of food to the people you like, but to poor people like me you give nothing."

God tried to argue with him, but the peasant gave nothing to God. So he went away.

Just as the peasant was going to eat the chicken, a thin, pale man came along. "Good morning, my friend," said the stranger. "Please give me something to eat."

"No, señor, I won't."

"Don't be unfair. I'm also hungry. You can spare a little piece of that chicken."

"No! It's all for me," the peasant cried out.

"But you don't know who I am."

"God just left here because I wouldn't give him any food. So who are you that you say I'll give you some?"

"I am Death!"

Now the peasant smiled and said, "You are right. I'll give you some chicken because you are just and fair. You treat everyone the same—rich and poor, fat and thin, young and old. With you I will share the chicken."

Two Different Kinds of Minds
by B. Pascal

Some people are good at mathematics. Their minds understand truths that are very obvious and clear. However, these are not the kinds of truths we come across in our daily ordinary experience. And, because of our usual habits, it is hard to turn our attention to truths of this sort. Other sorts of people have minds that grasp the truths of their daily lives without thinking. They are street-smart. They understand things by a kind of feeling. We call these people "intuitive." These truths of experience are in front of us all, but only some people have eyesight that is sharp enough to see them all since there are so many of them. And if you miss any one of these truths you'll make mistakes since they are all connected.

Those people good at math are used to very exact and simple truths and rules. These people don't reason well unless they can carefully arrange and order these truths. So they get lost when they try to think about their daily experience because the rules can't be arranged and organized exactly. We feel these truths of daily experience rather than think about them. Intuitive people seize a conclusion immediately rather than reach it through a process of reasoning. So it's very rare to find someone both good at mathematics and also intuitive. People good at mathematics appear silly because they try to think about their everyday experiences mathematically. They want to start with definitions and simple rules and reason from these. On the other hand, intuitive people who judge at a glance, are shocked when they look at a piece of mathematics. They can't understand why one has to start with definitions and carefully reason step-by-step to a conclusion. So these two types of people couldn't be more different.

The Histories
by Herodotus

Three Persians were arguing about the proper form of government for their country. The first spoke in favor of democracy. "Kingship is neither pleasant nor good. A king is permitted to do whatever he likes without any responsibility or control. Even the best person raised to such power would change for the worse. The evils of such a person are envy and pride. Absolute power in a king would seem to remove envy, but it doesn't. Kings become jealous of the best of their subjects, and take pleasure in their worst subjects. A king becomes furious if you do not bow down to him and yet despises you when you do. The rule of the people is entirely different. First, all are equal under the law. Secondly, people in office are responsible for what they do, and all questions are debated openly. So I propose that the people rule."

The second speaker spoke in favor of the rule by the few best citizens. "I agree that kingship is terrible but rule of the people is even worse. An entire people has no knowledge of government or affairs. A king does at least act thoughtfully, but the people do not. How could they since they never studied what is right and proper. The people rush into politics blindly like a river in flood. And rushing like a river, they are always on the verge of violence. We should choose the few best men and give them power. The best men will always choose the best policy."

The third and last speaker spoke in favor of a king. "Consider the three forms of government and think about the best of each kind and not the worst. If you do, you will choose kingship. If a man is the best possible man, he will be the best ruler. He will be constant in his judgments, he can keep secrets from the country's enemies, and he cannot be bribed. In the rule of a few, all men are competing for honors and the top position. Each wants to see his own suggestions followed. And since each is powerful and has followers, these personal conflicts become conflicts within the country. The only way out will be a king. Or consider democracy. Corruption is everywhere and groups of people create factions to gain something for themselves. This continues until it gets so bad that conflict breaks out and there is chaos. Then the people look for a champion to restore order and security. So this champion becomes a king. So we can see the other forms of government also lead to kingship. That should therefore be our form of government."

After these three speeches, the Persians chose their form of government. They chose to live under a king.

A Mathematician's Defense
By G. H. Hardy

A mathematician, like a painter or a poet, is a maker of patterns. If his patterns are more permanent than theirs, it is because his are made with ideas. A painter makes patterns with shapes and colors, a poet with words. A mathematician, on the other hand, works only with ideas. So his patterns are likely to last longer, since ideas don't wear out as quickly as words.

The mathematician's patterns, like the painter's or the poet's, must be beautiful. Beauty is the first test. It may be very hard to define mathematical beauty, but that's just as true of beauty of any kind. We may not be able to say what makes a poem beautiful, but we recognize one when we read it.

A chess problem is genuine mathematics, but it is in some way "trivial" mathematics. However clever and complicated, however original and surprising the moves, there is something essential lacking. Chess problems are unimportant. The best mathematics is serious as well as beautiful—"important" if you like, but "serious" is better.

I am not thinking of the "practical" consequences of mathematics. At present, I will say only that if a chess problem is, in the crude sense, useless, then that is equally true of most of the best mathematics. Very little of mathematics is useful practically, and that little is dull. The "seriousness" of a mathematical theorem lies not in its practical consequences which are usually slight. Instead, the seriousness of a theorem lies in the significance of the mathematical ideas it connects together. We may say, roughly, that a mathematical idea is "significant" if it can be connected, in a natural way, with a large body of other mathematical ideas. By this means the theorem is likely to lead to advances in mathematics itself, and even in the other sciences.

"You were blind and lame. How did you both survive?"

"We survived together," they said, "and now we can both see and walk. And we can all return to our village which is still standing."

So the two led the villagers back to their homes. If these two had not brought the people back, the villagers would never have seen their homes again.

Democracy in America
by A. de Tocqueville

Equality and Liberty

Everybody has noticed that an equality of living conditions for people produces a strong love of that equality. Every day this passion for equality is gaining ground among people everywhere. It has been said a hundred times that people in modern times are far more strongly attached to equality than to freedom.

It is possible to imagine an extreme point at which freedom and equality would meet and blend. Let us suppose that all the people take a part in the government, and that each one has an equal right to take part in it. Since no one is any different from anyone else, none of them can exercise tyrannical power. Everyone will be perfectly free because they are entirely equal. Everyone will be equal because they are entirely free. This would be an ideal democratic state. But there are a thousand others less perfect.

Equality may be established in society without existing in the political arena. For example, all the people may have equal rights to pursue the same pleasures, enter the same professions, go to the same places and seek wealth by the same means, yet not have an equal share in governing. Here we have equality without freedom.

It may indeed be true that mankind cannot be absolutely equal unless they are also free. Therefore equality, when pushed to the extreme, is often confused with freedom. Yet they are really quite different, and I am not afraid to add that among democratic nations they are two very different things. Freedom has often appeared in the world at different times and it is not only present in democracies. Freedom is not the characteristic of democracies. The special characteristic of democracies is a love for equality. This love for equality is the ruling passion of a democracy. Do not ask what special charm democratic people find in being equal, nor why they cling to it so strongly rather than other advantages society offers them. The fact is they prefer it to all the rest. Indeed, a democratic people will at all times prefer equality to freedom.

But because equality is so loved, it is exceedingly hard to destroy it once it is established in a state. Freedom, on the other hand, is more easily lost. To neglect to hold it fast is to allow it to escape.

10

The Consolation of Philosophy
by Boethius

Most people believe that either money, honor, power, or pleasure will make them happy. Let me show you briefly how each one of these contains something evil within itself. If you try to get money, you need to worry about keeping it, and must take more and more from others. If you receive honor from others, you owe a debt to those who give it to you. If you want more honor, you have to beg for it. If you get power, you risk being betrayed by those you have power over. If you seek fame, you lose your security and become involved in endless problems. If you seek a life of pleasure, you become dependent on the health of a weak and fragile thing—your body. For you're neither bigger than an elephant, nor stronger than a bull, nor faster than a tiger, and their bodies wear away.

Look up at the stars, and consider the size and the stability of the heavens, and stop admiring base things. Your own beauty passes away swiftly, even faster than that of the spring flowers. If we had eyes which could see through stone walls, wouldn't we find a beautiful body ugly when we saw the stomach, the liver, and all our insides. So it is not your own nature which makes you look beautiful, but the weak eyes of the other people who look at you. Admire your body as much as you like, but remember that what you admire so much can be destroyed by a slight fever which lasts only a few days.

All these arguments can be summed up in one truth: money, honor, power, and pleasure are all limited. They make us believe they will make us happy, but they can't give happiness to us.

What incredible ignorance drives miserable men along these crooked paths! You don't look for gold in trees or for jewels growing on bushes. If you want a fish for dinner, you don't cast your nets up in high mountains. If you want to hunt deer, you don't go to the ocean. No, we are skilled in knowing the hidden caves in the sea; we know where pearls and precious gems are found. We know which lakes and waters have which fish. But when it comes to looking for the good which everyone wants, people are blind and ignorant. They look in places where they should know they will never find happiness. What can I say to show them what fools they are? Let them seek money, honor, power, fame and pleasure. When they have painfully gotten what they wanted, they may finally see their mistake and learn that these goods are all false.

Declaration of Independence
(Opening Paragraphs)

When in the course of human events it becomes necessary for one people to dissolve the political bonds which have connected them with another, and to assume among the powers of the earth the separate and equal station to which the laws of nature and of nature's god *entitle*[1] them, a decent respect to the opinions of mankind requires that they should declare the causes which *impel*[2] them to the separation.

We hold these truths to be *self-evident*[3]: that all men are created equal; that they are *endowed*[4] by their Creator with certain *inalienable*[5] rights; that among these are life, liberty, and the pursuit of happiness.

[1] give them.
[2] urge.
[3] to be obvious if you think about it.
[4] provided.
[5] rights which cannot be taken or given away.

On Public Education
by Thomas Jefferson

Another of our purposes in this Constitution is to spread knowledge more generally through the mass of people. We propose to divide every county into small districts, each about five or six miles square. Each district will have a school for teaching reading, writing, and arithmetic. Each district is responsible for paying teachers, and every person in the district may send their children free for three years; longer if they pay for it.

A special person called a Visitor will choose from each school the best student who will be sent on to grammar school for six years free of charges to study Greek, Latin, geography, and higher arithmetic. At the end of the six years, by means of trials or exams, the best half of the students will be sent on to William and Mary College to study for three years such subjects as they choose, all at public expense. The remaining half will be dismissed and encouraged to teach at the grammar schools.

The result of this is that, from the whole population, all children will be able to read, write, and do common arithmetic. A smaller fraction of the citizens will be well versed in Greek, Latin, geography, and higher branches of arithmetic. Of this fraction, one half will be educated yet further at William and Mary College to study advanced sciences and subjects.

All of this is at public expense, but for those who are able and willing to pay the costs themselves, the schools are available to educate their children.

Continuity and Irrational Numbers
by Richard Dedekind

I regard the whole of arithmetic as a necessary, or at least natural, consequence of the simplest arithmetic act, that of counting. Counting itself is nothing more than the successive creation of the infinite series of numbers, in which each new number is defined by the one immediately preceding it. The simplest act of counting is the passing from an already-formed individual number to the consecutive new one to be formed—going from 4 to 5. The chain of these numbers is an exceedingly useful instrument for the human mind. It presents an inexhaustible wealth of remarkable laws obtained by the introduction of the four fundamental operations of arithmetic—addition, multiplication, subtraction, and division. Addition is the combination of any arbitrary repetitions of the above-mentioned simplest act into a single act. Adding 2 + 4 means counting up to 2 and then counting 4 more from there. In a similar way, multiplication arises from counting.

While addition and multiplication are always possible with counting numbers, the inverse operations, subtraction and division, prove to be limited. For instance, if we are asked to subtract 5 from 3, the counting numbers do not give us an answer. Likewise, if we try to divide 3 by 5, the counting numbers again cannot provide an answer.

Whatever the immediate occasion may have been, it is certainly true that this limitation in performing the indirect operations of subtraction and division has in each case been the real motive for a new creative act. The problem of subtraction led to the creation of negative numbers, (3-5 = -2), while the problem of division led to fractions (3 divided by 5 = 3/5). Thus negative and fractional numbers have been created by the human mind. As a group, counting numbers, negative numbers, and fractions make up what we call the rational numbers. With these rational numbers, which result from these two creative acts, there has been gained a tool of infinitely greater perfection than just the counting numbers we previously had.

Character
by Voltaire

Character comes from the Greek word for "impression" and "engraving." It is what nature has carved and engraved in us. Can we erase or change it? If I have a bent nose and two cat-like eyes, I can hide them behind a mask. Do I have more power or even as much over the character nature has given me?

A man born violent and hot-headed comes before King Francis I of France to complain about an injury. The appearance of the king, the respectful behavior of those near the king, and the size of the palace make a very powerful impression on this man. He lowers his eyes, his coarse voice becomes soft. He presents his petition humbly. One would think him as gentle as those courtiers who always go with the king. He is even confused while he is in this strange and unfamiliar place. But if the king can read faces, he will know everything he needs to know about this man. The king will easily discover in the lowered eyes a deep fire. By seeing the tightened muscles of this man's face and his lips pressed against each other, the king will realize that the man is not as gentle as he is forced to appear. But the king doesn't notice these signs.

This man follows the king to war and both are taken prisoner and thrown in jail. In prison, the king no longer makes the same kind of impression on the man. He begins to lose respect for the king. One day, while he is pulling off the king's boots and pulling them off badly, the king, made bitter by misfortune, becomes angry. The man's violent temper comes back. He attacks the king, gets rid of him, and throws his boots out the window. As the Roman writer Horace said, "Drive out nature with a pitchfork, she'll always return."

Religion and ethics put a curb on nature's strength but they cannot destroy it. The drunkard in a hospital, reduced to cider with his meals, will not get drunk any more. But he will always love wine.

Anger weakens character. Character is like a tree, which, when it grows old, produces bad fruit but still of the same kind it used to produce. The tree becomes covered with knots and moss, becomes worm eaten, but it remains an oak or a pear tree. If we could change our character, if we could give ourselves one, we would be the master of nature. Can we give ourselves anything? Don't we receive everything? Try to stir up a lazy man with regular activity. Try to cool the boiling soul of someone who is reckless. Try to inspire the man who lacks taste or an ear with feeling for music and poetry. You would find it easier to give sight to a man born blind. We can improve, we can smooth down, we can hide what nature has placed in us. But we can put nothing there ourselves.

On Moral Education
by Horace Mann

The uncontrolled passions of mankind are not only homicidal, but suicidal; and a community without control would soon destroy itself. Even with a conscience, evil often triumphs over good. As the relations between people become more complex, and the business of the world more extended, new opportunities and temptations for wrongdoing have been created. Following the loving relations of parent and child came murder within a family. Following a duty to speak the truth came lies and perjury. Following relations between tribes and nations came war and slavery. The government puts a tax on imported goods, smugglers hide the goods and lie to inspectors to make more money. Science discovers a new medicine to ease pain or cure diseases, criminals abuse it or imitate it with a cheap substitute and sell it at a huge profit. In short, all laws designed to repress injustice and crime give rise to new injustices and crimes to avoid the first.

Now, how shall this flood of immoralities and crimes be stemmed?

The human race has existed long enough to have tried many experiments to solve this great problem. Mankind have tried tyrants, kings, mob rule, no rule, and execution for the smallest offense. They have tried rule by religious authority, they have imprisoned, burnt, and slaughtered not only individuals but whole communities at a time. None has succeeded or lasted for very long.

But there is one experiment which has never yet been tried. Education has never been brought to bear with the one hundredth part of its possible force upon the natures of children and, through them, upon the character of adults and the whole race. We all understand the roots of the power of education. It is expressed in these few words: *"Train up a child in the way he should go, and when he is old he will not depart from it."* This is a positive statement. If the first part is done correctly, the second will follow without fail. Although it deals with morals, its result is as sure as a chemical experiment.

Here, then, is a new agency, the educational system, whose mighty powers have only been weakly used. Yet we know that it could be more far-reaching and decisive than any other earthly instrument.

16 The Notebooks
by Leonardo da Vinci

Painting and Poetry

Painting is better than all other human works because it contains so many possibilities.

We get most of our knowledge of the world through our eyes. Our ears are in second place. They only hear about the things the eye has seen. If poets, historians, and mathematicians had not seen things with their eyes, they would not be able to describe them in their writings. A painter with his brushes can tell a story much better than a poet with his pen. He can make it more interesting and easier to understand. A poet can call painting "poetry without a voice," but a painter can call poetry "blind painting." Which is better, to be without a voice or to be blind? A poet has to use words to describe shapes, actions, and scenes. A painter can make the exact images of these. Which is more important, the shape or the name? The name changes, the shape is unchanged except by death.

Let me give an example. If a painter and a poet both describe a great battle, which will be the most interesting? Show them in public side by side, and you will see to which people are drawn. More people will go to the painting and discuss it, and praise it. The painting will give people greater pleasure, because it is more beautiful and useful. Also, imagine a poet describing a lady's beauty to her lover, and a painter painting a picture of her. To which, the poem or the painting, will the lover become more attached? Experience provides the proof of the matter.

Some people say that painting is inferior because it is a mechanical art. They say that the painter has to use his hands and his brushes to represent what his imagination creates. But, doesn't the writer also have to put down in writing, with pen and paper, what he is thinking about? Other people say painting is inferior because it is done for money. But, don't teachers in schools also go where the pay is best? Does anyone work without pay?

Painters are like the grandsons of God. Poets describe the working of the human mind, painting describes what the mind accomplishes by using the body. The poet can describe a horrible thing, but the painter can show it to you. Which is the more realistic? Haven't we all seen paintings which are so much like the actual thing that both men and animals have been fooled by them? Painting is a science, because it can show us all the visible things in the world: plants, animals, grass and flowers, all surrounded by light and shade. Whoever doesn't appreciate painting, doesn't appreciate nature, because painting is like a child of nature and since nature was created by God, it is like a grandchild of God.

Article One of the Amendments to The Constitution of the United State

*Freedom of Religion, of Speech,
of the Press, of assembly, and of petition*

Congress shall make no law respecting an establishment of religion, or prohibiting the free exercise thereof; or abridging the freedom of speech, or of the press; or the right of the people peaceably to assemble, and to petition the government for a redress of grievances.

18
On Religion and the State
by Thomas Jefferson

Should different religions be permitted in our State?

In October 1776, the convention met as a member of the general assembly and repealed and overturned all previous acts of parliament. Several earlier acts of the Virginia Assembly, in 1659, 1662, and 1693, had made it a crime for parents to refuse to baptize their children and for Quakers to gather together. Quakers were forced out of Virginia, imprisoned if they returned once or twice, and executed on the third time.

By our own act of assembly of 1705, if a person brought up in the Christian religion denies the being of God, or the Trinity, or says there are more gods than one, or denies the Christian religion to be true, or the scriptures to be of divine authority, he is punished by not being allowed to hold any office or employment in the government or the military. If he breaks these laws twice, he is not allowed to sue anyone in court, nor inherit anything, and is imprisoned for three years. His children are taken away and given to others to guard and raise. This is a brief summary of the religious slavery under which we have been living here in Virginia and which we have overthrown by our repealing of those acts of parliament in 1776 which we spoke of above.

It is our view now that our rulers should only make laws over our natural rights which we submit to them. We never submitted our rights of conscience to our rulers. We answer for them only to God. The legitimate powers of government only cover acts which injure others. It does me no injury for my neighbor to say there are twenty gods or no gods. Such beliefs do not pick my pocket nor break my leg. Putting my neighbor in prison will not change his mind, though it may make him say what I want him to say and so become a hypocrite.

Reason and free inquiry are the only effective cures for error. Let them loose and they will support true beliefs by bringing all false ones to the test of their investigation. Reason and free inquiry are the natural enemies of error, and of error only. When reason and experiment are indulged and allowed full free reign, error flees before them. It is error alone that needs the support of government. Truth can stand by itself.

Federalist Paper No. 10
by James Madison

Among the many advantages of a well-formed Union of all the States, none deserves more attention than its tendency to control violence among factions. By a faction I mean a number of citizens—either a majority of them or a minority of them—who group themselves together and who are motivated by some common interest or cause. But this common interest or cause is opposed to and threatens the rights of other citizens or the interests of the community as a whole.

There are two ways of removing the causes of faction. One of them is by destroying the freedom which is essential for factions to exist in the first place. The other way is to make sure that every citizen has the same opinions, the same passions, and the same interests.

Nothing is more true than that the first cure—to destroy the freedom of everyone—is far worse than the disease; that is, factions fighting each other. Liberty is to faction as air is to fire. But it would be as foolish to destroy liberty, which is essential to healthy political life, as it would be to destroy air, which is necessary for any animal life, simply because it also allows fire to exist.

The second cure—to make sure every citizen has the same opinions—is impossible. As long as the reason of human beings continues to make mistakes sometimes and people are free to use their reason, there will be different opinions on all kinds of matters. As long as the connection continues existing between one's reason and self-love, they will constantly affect each other.

So, that which lies behind the causes of faction is part of the very nature of mankind. The energy which produces different opinions concerning religion, government, and many other points and which makes us follow different leaders—that same energy divides human beings into factions. It inflames them to dislike and hate one another. It makes them much more likely to oppress and fight one another than to work for their common good.

It is because of the energy of this self-love and self-interest that no one is allowed to be a judge in one's own cause. It is even more certain that a group of people—a faction—should not be lawmakers, judge, and jury in their own cause at the same time.

From this it follows that a pure democracy, by which I mean a small society who try to govern themselves in person, will never cure the evils of faction. The majority will always rule over, and oppress, the minority. But a republic, by which I mean a government in which a scheme of representation takes place, promises a cure for which we are looking.

The two main differences between a democracy and a republic are: first, that in a republic, the government is a small number of citizens elected by all the citizens; secondly, a republic can extend over a very large country and very many citizens.

The effect of these differences is that the many different opinions of the masses from all over the country will be refined by passing them through the medium of the representatives, chosen by all the citizens. These representatives are more likely to be wise enough to see better the true interest of their country and less likely to sacrifice it to some temporary considerations.

In the next place, in a large republic, each representative will be chosen by a large number of citizens, and so it will be more difficult for unworthy candidates to cheat at getting elected. Again, since the people are more free, they will be more likely to elect a person of attractive and stable character.

Federalist Paper No. 2
by John Jay

Nothing is more certain than the necessity for government. It is equally sure that in order to set up any government, people are required to give to it some of their natural rights; for the government requires some powers which only the people possess and can give to it. It is now necessary that we ask whether America would be better as one single nation or as a collection of independent but related States.

It has often given me pleasure to think that a whole, independent, united America is not made up of detached parts which are held at a distance from each other. Rather, I think of it as one connected, rich and vast country. Providence has specially blessed it with a variety of soils and watered it with very many streams and rivers. These rivers and ports around the coasts, along with good highways, form a complex network which makes easy communication and commerce possible.

With equal pleasure I have often noted that Providence has given this one connected country to one united people—a people descended from the same ancestors, speaking the same language, professing the same religion, attached to the same principles of government, very similar in their manners and customs, and who have just fought a long and bloody war to establish their freedom and independence.

This country and this people seem to have been made for each other. It appears that it is part of a great plan that this band of brothers, united to each other by such strong ties as language, religion, and custom, should never be split into a number of unsocial, jealous, and hostile entities or separate states.

21
Democracy in America
by Alexis de Tocqueville

Why Americans are so Restless

In certain remote parts of the Old World, you can find people living who are extremely ignorant and poor. They take no part in the business of their country and are often oppressed by their government, yet their faces are peaceful and their spirits light.

In America I saw the freest and most enlightened people placed in happy circumstances, but it seemed that they had a dark cloud hanging over them. They seemed serious and sad, even in their pleasures.

The chief reason for this difference between the two peoples is that the first group does not think of the hardships they endure while Americans are always brooding over pleasures and benefits they do not possess. Americans pursue their goals with feverish work and are constantly in dread that they have lost time in chasing their goal.

Americans quickly grasp everything within reach as though afraid they might not live long enough to enjoy them. They grab everything but soon loosen their grasp in order to pursue fresh pleasures.

In the United States, a person builds a house in which to spend his old age, yet he sells it before the roof is on. He plants a garden but leaves it before it bears fruit. He learns how to earn a living, but gives it up before starting a job. After a year's work he gets a few days' vacation, so he will travel many hundreds of miles to become unhappy again. Death finally comes to him, but it is before he is tired of the aimless chase of happiness and quiet which forever escapes him.

It is the American taste for physical pleasures that is the cause of the secret urge for action. People who set their hearts on the pursuit of worldly goods are always in a hurry, for there is only a limited time to reach, to grasp, and to enjoy it. In addition to the goods an American is enjoying now, he is constantly imagining a thousand others that death will prevent him from trying if he does not try them soon. This thought fills him with anxiety and fear and constantly leads him to change his plans and goals.

The Meno
by Plato

Socrates: What if someone asked you: "What is shape?" and you replied that roundness is shape. Wouldn't he then ask you as I did, "Do you mean roundness is shape or a shape?" And wouldn't you reply, of course that it is a shape.

Meno: Certainly.

Socrates: Your reason being that there are other shapes as well.

Meno: Yes.

Socrates: And if he went on to ask you what they were, you would tell him that squares and triangles are also shapes. Seeing that you call these many particular things by one and the same name, and that you say that every one of them is a shape, even though they are the contrary of each other, what is it that embraces round as well as straight-lined figures? What do you mean by shape when you say that a straight-lined figure has a shape as much as a round one. You do say that, don't you?

Meno: Yes.

Socrates: And in saying it, do you mean that a round figure is no more round than it is straight, and a straight-lined figure no more straight than round?

Meno: Of course not.

Socrates: Yet you do say that a round figure is no more a shape than a straight-sided one and the other way about.

Meno: Quite true.

Socrates: Then what is this thing called "shape"? Try to tell me. If when asked this question either about shape or color you said, "But I don't understand what you want, or what you mean," your questioner would perhaps be surprised and say, "Don't you see that I am looking for what is the same in all of them?" Would you be unable to reply, if the question was, "What is it that is common to round figures like circles and straight lined figures like squares and triangles and the other things which you call shapes?" Do your best to answer.

Meno: No, you do it, Socrates.

23 Prisoners Listening to Music
by Kathe Kollwitz

24
To Emancipate the Mind
by Abraham Lincoln, 1859

Speech alone has not advanced the condition of the world much. *Writing*—the art of communicating thoughts to the mind through the eye—is the great invention of the world. It enables us to converse with the dead, the absent, and the unborn, at all distances of time and of space. It is great, not only in its direct benefits, but also in comparison to all other inventions.

When we remember that words are merely *sounds*, we shall conclude that the idea of representing those sounds by *marks* was a bold and ingenious conception, not likely to occur to one man of a million in the run of a thousand years. An even greater step was making a mark, not to represent a whole sound, but only a part of one, and then of combining these marks, not very many in number, so as to represent any and all words. This was the invention of *phonetic* writing, as distinguished from the clumsy picture writing of some of the older nations. The difficulty of conceiving and executing this invention is apparent. Its utility may be conceived by the reflection that to *it* we owe everything which distinguishes us from savages. Take writing from us, and the Bible, all history, all science, all government, all commerce, and nearly all social interaction go with it.

I have already intimated my opinion that in the world's history, certain inventions and discoveries occurred, of peculiar value, on account of their great efficiency in facilitating all other inventions and discoveries. Of these were the arts of writing and of printing. But, to return to the consideration of printing, it is plain that it is but the *other* half—and in real utility, the better half—of writing and that both together are but the assistants of speech in the communication of thoughts between man and man. When man was possessed of speech alone, the chances of invention, discovery, and improvement were very limited. But by the introduction of each of these, the prospects of new inventions and improvements were greatly multiplied. When writing was invented, any important observation, likely to lead to a discovery, had at least a chance of being written down. By this means, the observation of a single individual might lead to an important invention, years, and even centuries after he was dead. And yet, for the three thousand years during which printing remained undiscovered after writing was in use, it was only a small portion of the people who could write or read and, consequently, the field of invention, though much extended, still continued very limited.

At length printing came. It gave ten thousand copies of any written matter, quite as cheaply as ten were given before, and consequently a thousand minds were brought into the field where there was but one before. It is very probable—almost certain—that the great mass of men, at that time, were utterly unconscious that their *conditions*, or their *minds*, were capable of improvement. They not only looked upon the educated few as superior beings but they supposed themselves to be naturally incapable of rising to equality. To emancipate the mind from this false perception of itself is the great task which printing came into the world to perform. It is difficult for us, *now* and *here*, to conceive how strong this slavery of the mind was and how long it did, of necessity, take to break its shackles and to get a habit of freedom of thought established.

25
Bonifacius—Essays to Do Good
by Cotton Mather

Neighbors! You are connected one to another. And the way you behave should make everyone in the neighborhood glad they live there. We read, "A righteous person is better than his neighbor." But we don't think so, unless he is better as a neighbor. He must excel in being a good neighbor.

First: the poor people who lie wounded must have their wounds cared for and healed. A modern prince was recently told, "To be in need is to deserve his favor." Good neighbor, put on that royal quality! See who in the neighborhood may deserve your favor. We are told: "This is pure religion—to pay visits to the widows in their need and to those who have no father." The orphans and widows, and all children in need of help should be visited and given the help they need.

Neighbors! Care for the orphans and widows in your neighborhood. They meet great difficulties and are often tempted to do wrong. While their relatives were alive, they may have been poorly provided for but at least they had something. How much worse off must they be now they are alone? Think about it, and this should be the result: "I helped the children who had no helper and caused the widow to sing with joy." In this way, each and every person in the neighborhood is thought about. Would it be too much for you at least once a week to think "Which of my neighbors is reduced to penny-pinching and painful poverty?" Think "Who is heartbroken with a sad death in the family?" And think: "Which neighbor's soul is being tempted to evil, or being hurt in some way?" But then think: "What shall be done for such neighbors?"

First: You will pity them. "Have compassion for one another—be pitiful." This has always been, and always will be, justly expected of you. Let our pity for them burst out into a prayer for them. It would be a fine practice for you, in your private daily prayers to think, "What misery have I seen today that I may do well now to ask for the mercy of the Lord."

But this is not all. Probably, you should visit them, and when you visit, comfort them. Carry to them some good word that may make their sad heart more glad.

And lastly: Give them assistance that will help them in their misery. Assist them with advice, assist them with greetings from other people. If it is necessary, give them what they need: "Give bread to the hungry; offer them shelter in your house; give clothes to those who are naked or in rags." At least, I beg of you, "If you have nothing else to give to the poor and wretched, give a tear or two for their misery." This is better than nothing.

As you consider what helps make a good neighborhood, the main principle I would have you keep in mind is that you look to the spiritual needs of your neighborhood as well as their material needs. Be concerned that lies and temptations do not make your neighbors commit sins. If there are lazy persons, I beg you, cure them of their idleness. Find them work; set them to work; keep them to work.

26
Emile or On Education
by Jean-Jacques Rousseau

Do you know the most likely way to make your children unhappy? You can make them unhappy by giving them everything they want. When it is so easy for them to get what they want, they want more and more things. They will want your hat, your watch, and even the birds in the air. So sooner or later, because you can't keep up with them, you will have to say, "No." This will cause more pain than if you had not tried to give them everything they had wanted. Such children believe they own the world. They think all people are their slaves. When you try to explain why you finally said "No," they think it's just an excuse. They feel they have been wronged and hurt by you. They begin to hate everyone. They are never grateful. They never thank anyone.

Could such a child ever be happy? No. They are tyrants. I have seen children raised this way fill the air with their cries the moment they are not obeyed. They complain all the time. They beat on the table. And what are they like when they grow up and go out into the world or start school? There, they are surprised when they don't get their own way. In the world, people don't jump to get them what they want. They thought everything was theirs, and now they can't understand what has happened. They become afraid and mixed up and begin to feel they are very weak. When they were younger, they felt they could do anything. Now, they feel they can do nothing. Nature has made children to be loved and helped. But should we fear and obey them?

Open Letter to His Former Master
by Frederick Douglass

Thomas Auld:

Sir—The long and intimate, though by no means friendly relation which unhappily existed between you and myself, leads me to hope that you will easily account for the great liberty which I now take in addressing you in this open and public manner.

I have selected this day on which to address you, because it is the anniversary of my emancipation; and knowing of no better way, I am led to this as the best mode of celebrating that truly important event. Just ten years ago this beautiful September morning, yon bright sun beheld me a slave—a poor, degraded chattel—trembling at the sound of your voice, lamenting that I was a man, and wishing myself a brute. You, Sir, can never know my feelings. As I look back to them, I can scarcely realize that I have passed through a scene so trying.

Oh! Sir, a slave-holder never appears to me so completely an agent of hell, as when I think of and look upon my dear children. It is then that my feelings rise above my control. I meant to have said more with respect to my own prosperity and happiness, but thoughts and feelings which this recital has awakened unfit me to proceed further in that direction: the grim direction! The grim horrors of slavery rise in all their ghastly terror before me, the wails of millions pierce my heart, and chill my blood.

At this moment, you are probably the guilty holder of at least three of my own dear sisters, and my only brother in bondage. These you regard as your property. They are recorded on your ledger and perhaps are still filling your own ever-hungry purse by their work. Sir, I desire to know how and where these dear sisters are. Let me know all about them. I would write to them, and learn all I want to know of them, without disturbing you in any way, but that, through your unrighteous conduct, they have been entirely deprived of the power to read and write. You have kept them in utter ignorance, and have therefore robbed them of the sweet enjoyments of writing or receiving letters from absent friends and relatives.

I will now bring this letter to a close; you shall hear from me again unless you let me hear from you. I intend to make use of you as a weapon with which to assail the system of slavery; as a means of concentrating public attention on the system and deepening their horror of trafficking in the souls and bodies of men. I shall make use of you as a means of bringing this guilty nation with yourself to repentance. In doing this I entertain no malice towards you personally. There is no roof under which you would be more safe than mine, and there is nothing in my house which you might need for your comfort, which I would not readily grant. Indeed, I should esteem it a privilege, to set you an example as to how mankind ought to treat each other.

I am your fellow man, but not your slave.
Frederick Douglass

28
The Life of Alcibiades
by Plutarch

Alcibiades was born into a very wealthy family of Athens. Not only did they have great wealth, but there were many generations of nobility on both his mother's and especially on his father's side. When he was still a young man, he was made a general in the army and, with great skill won several victories. Soon after that, because the Athenians accused him of being disrespectful to their gods, he went over to the Athenian's enemy, the Spartans, and helped them wage war on Athens. Here are two stories about Alcibiades when he was a young child.

Once, he was being badly beaten as he was wrestling with another boy. He was afraid he would soon be thrown to the ground, so he bit the other boy on the hand as hard as he could. The other boy let Alcibiades loose and cried out, "You bite like a woman." "No," said Alcibiades. "I bite like a lion." Another time as he was playing at dice in the street, a loaded cart came down the street just as he was about to throw the dice. He called to the driver to stop because the cart would have got in his way. But the driver ignored him. So Alcibiades threw himself in front of the horse which made the driver pull on the reins to stop the horse. Everyone who saw what happened rushed to help Alcibiades and make sure he wasn't hurt.

As he was growing up, many of those of his own age and also many who were even older flattered him and furthered his career.

At the young age of eighteen, he became a general in the army. After leading the Athenian army with skill and daring, Alcibiades was found guilty of a serious religious offense. He immediately left Athens and offered his skill and services to the enemy, the Spartans. When the Spartans later became dissatisfied with him and did not pay him the respect he thought he deserved, he left and joined a common enemy, the Persians. Everywhere he went he had this talent of gaining affection, for he quickly imitated the habits and ways of life of whomever he was with. Alcibiades could adapt himself to his company and equally give the appearance of being good or bad as he wished. At Sparta, he seemed to love physical exercise and living with very little money. In Ionia, he lived in luxury and lazily. In Thessaly, he was always on horseback. In Thrace, he was always drinking wine. In Persia, he appeared more magnificent and royal than the Persians. He adopted any fashion and form that made him most acceptable and agreeable to those who were with him.

29
Woman Holding a Balance
by Jan Vermeer

(Please see page 73 for the artwork.)

We Cannot Live for Ourselves Alone
by Vernon E. Jordan Jr.

For just as no man is an island, separate and apart from others, so too, no community can see itself in isolation from other towns and cities, from the nation as a whole, or from countries and people far from our borders. In our times especially, we have seen how racial and economic problems penetrate even the most self-contained rich communities. We have seen the problems of rural poverty and racism become the core problems of our urban crises. Now we see them becoming part of suburban life as well.

There is no hiding place in the modern world. There can be no isolation from social problems. If our society is to grow and prosper, if our civilization is to flourish, then indeed our voluntary agencies must be directed to ensuring the equality toward which we have strived.

This is not to de-emphasize the proper role of government. Because government has great resources legal powers of persuasion and is politically accountable, it must hold a central position in organizing our society's efforts toward political, social, and economic equality.

True self-interest has to do not only with looking out for yourself, but also with the preservation of society's goals and values, and with the creation of conditions in which all people may get ahead and share in the responsibilities of citizenship. Neglect of this true self-interest leads, as we have seen, to racial conflict, to poverty and the bitterness that comes with poverty, and to the breakdown of rules of conduct and civilized behavior.

What is so often called the urban crises or the racial crises is often nothing more than the result of people confusing selfishness with true self-interest.

It is clear to me that the spirit of true self-interest and of volunteer work as a means of changing our society are very important to our nation's future. And linked to this concept of creative volunteerism is the need to encourage voluntary activity among all people and not to restrict participation in volunteer work to those with time and money.

At the center of a positive response must be the understanding that we are all linked together in such a way that our efforts to help others make our own lives more satisfying and more secure.

Lesson 29, *Woman Holding a Balance*

Made in the USA